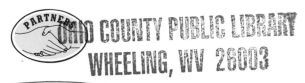

BILL PHIL
BOWERMAN & KNIGHT
BUILDING THE NIKE EMPIRE

BY
Keith Elliot Greenberg
Illustrations by Dick Smolinski

 A BLACKBIRCH PRESS BOOK

WOODBRIDGE, CONNECTICUT

Published by Blackbirch Press, Inc.
One Bradley Road
Woodbridge , CT 06525

©1994 Blackbirch Press, Inc.
First Edition

Printed in Hong Kong

10 9 8 7 6 5 4 3 2 1

Information for this book came from Nike promotional materials, the book *Swoosh: The Unauthorized Story of Nike and the Men Who Played There*, by J.B. Strasser and Laurie Becklund, and the following publications: *Harvard Business Review, US News & World Report, Business Week, Runner's World, Financial World, Reader's Digest, Forbes, People* and *Vanity Fair.*

Library of Congress Cataloging-in-Publication Data

Greenberg, Keith Elliot.
    Philip Knight and John Bowerman: building the Nike empire / by Keith Elliot Greenberg.
      p.   cm. — (Partners)
    Includes bibliographical references and index.
    ISBN 1-56711-085-1   ISBN 1-56711-117-3 (Pbk.)
    1. Knight, Philip H., 1938–   —Juvenile literature. 2. Bowerman, William J.—Juvenile literature. 3. Nike (Firm)—Juvenile literature. 4. Businessmen—United States—Juvenile literature. [1. Knight, Philip H. 1938– . 2. Bowerman, William J. 3.Businessmen. 4. Nike (Firm)—History.] I. Title. II. Series.
HD9992.U52K554 1994
338.7'68536—dc20
                                       94-12747
                                          CIP
                                          AC

~ Contents ~

Chapter 1. **Just Do It!** 5

Chapter 2. **Coming Together** 9

Chapter 3. **Chasing a Dream** 20

Chapter 4. **Building on an Idea** 25

Chapter 5. **The Birth of Nike** 31

Chapter 6. **Ups and Downs** 36

Chapter 7. **Moving Forward** 41

Glossary 47

Further Reading 47

Index 48

Phil Knight and Bill Bowerman turned their love for running into one of the most successful sports companies in the world.

Just Do It!

"Bo Knows." "There Is No Finish Line." "Just Do It." Many people around the world know these slogans for Nike sneakers. These catchy phrases have convinced hundreds of thousands of customers to buy the products that Nike makes. But the founders of Nike have always wanted their company to do more than sell sneakers. They hope it also expresses an attitude.

Co-founder Phil Knight believes that, above all things, Nike encourages excellence. "Nike stands for performance," he says.

Phil learned about performance from his college track coach—and Nike co-founder—Bill Bowerman. Bill taught his athletes not only how to win races, but also how to succeed in life.

Bill was coach at the University of Oregon from 1948 to 1973. There, he brought the track team to four National Collegiate Athletic Association (NCAA) championships. Eleven of his athletes competed in the Olympics. Many others went on to become Nike's best salesmen. In 1972, Bill was named head coach of the U.S. Olympic track squad.

But Bill Bowerman was more than a coach—he was also an author and inventor. His 1967 book on jogging helped to create a running craze in America. And his sneaker designs made Nike into the number one sports-and-fitness company in the world.

Today, as Nike's head, Phil constantly thinks of his old coach's lessons. Phil's friends often say that he still looks at the world from the point of view of a track athlete. "This is a guy who chases dreams and catches them," said a former employee. "I have never seen him look back, even when he goes for a run."

Starting a Company Together

In 1964, Phil Knight and Bill Bowerman were both looking toward the future. They each chipped in $500 to start a company with an office in Phil's

In 1964, Phil and Bill set up their first company in Phil's mother's laundry room.

mother's laundry room. "We have come a long way," Phil said in a recent interview. "But we have not come as far as we have yet to go."

Today, Nike is headquartered in seven buildings on 74 acres in Beaverton, Oregon. Annual sales are more than $3.5-billion. Nike products are found in 100 countries.

What makes Nike so special in the world of fitness? Phil has said that the company tries to always listen to the needs of its users: "When we were just a running shoe company, almost all our employees were runners...We and the consumer were one and the same.

"When we started making shoes for basketball, tennis, and football, we did essentially the same thing we did in running. We got to know the players at the top of the game and did everything we could to understand what they needed."

The company tries to listen to the needs of its users.

The story of Nike is the unique story of the partnership between Phil Knight and Bill Bowerman. At first, Bill was the teacher and Phil was the student. Then, Phil became the businessman while his former coach developed new sneakers. Nike quickly became one of the world's most popular companies—partly because of its special approach to advertising but mostly because both partners loved the products they sold so much.

"I can't say that I would be that passionate about cigarettes and beer," Phil explains. "But that's why I'm not doing cigarettes and beer."

~ 2 ~

Coming Together

Despite an age difference of 26 years, Philip H. Knight and Bill Bowerman have always shared a love for running, and a constant desire to achieve excellence.

Phil is described by old friends as shy. Many of them say that, as a child, he didn't seem like the type of person who would one day gain fame. His college roommate—and fellow track team member—remembers, "I would not have thought he had this tremendous future ahead of him. That comes as a great surprise."

But what Phil—or "Buck," as his friends called him—had was determination. Once he found something he believed in, he usually did well at it.

Oregon Roots

Phil was born in 1938 in the Portland, Oregon, suburb of Eastmoreland. While his mother, Lota, tended to the home, his father, William W. Knight, showed some of the leadership Phil would later inherit. At the young age of 26, William Knight was elected to the Oregon state legislature. Later, he became a successful lawyer, representing newspaper publishers, among other clients. In 1953, when an airplane crash killed the publisher of the *Oregon Journal*, the widow chose Phil's father to take over.

At the age of 15, Phil was on his way to making a name for himself at Cleveland High School. He was described in the yearbook as one of the most "pleasant" students in the 1955 graduating class. He made the honor roll, played tennis, and ran track. Over time, he became one of the city's best middle-distance runners.

Phil decided to attend his father's college, the University of Oregon in the town of Eugene. One of the attractions was Bill Bowerman, then considered to be one of the best track coaches in the country. It's been said that Bill changed Eugene from a typical logging community to the country's track capital.

While in high school, Phil distinguished himself as one of Oregon's best runners.

The Making of a Coach

Bill was raised in the tradition of the hardy pioneers who settled Oregon. In fact, his great grandfather had ridden the rugged Oregon Trail to the unsettled west in the 1840s.

When Bill was seven, his mother Lizzie—a teacher—moved the family from the small town of Fossil to Medford, Oregon. Lizzie believed her child could have a better education there. Indeed, at Medford High School, Bill shined in numerous areas. He played the clarinet and edited the school newspaper. In 1928, he starred on the school's state championship football team.

Bill's wife Barbara recalls how, when they met in high school, Bill "was the most determined person I ever met. He would do anything to win."

Lizzie Bowerman later moved from Medford to Eugene to run a boarding house. Bill helped out his mother there, while studying business and medicine at the University of Oregon. He also found the time to own and manage a gas station.

Bill didn't discover running until his sophomore year. The first time he saw a one-mile race, he realized how exciting track could be. He introduced

In 1928, Bill starred on his high school's championship football team.

himself to the college's now legendary coach, Bill Hayward, and said he wanted to compete. Hayward admired the boy's dedication and agreed to teach him about track. Bill says that Hayward's lessons made him the fastest member of the football team.

13

The Power of Positive Thinking

The experience showed Bill Bowerman how much could be gained by positive thinking. That message would later be given to the athletes he coached. One day, he'd apply Hayward's philosophy to Nike.

"Everything I've ever done, I owe to Bill Hayward," Bill Bowerman has said.

After college, Bill started coaching football and track at Medford High. He said that he would only stay for a year, before going to medical school. But something about leading young men appealed to Bill, and he couldn't bring himself to leave. Then Bill's old coach encouraged Bill to focus his energies on running. "There are dozens of outstanding football coaches in the country," he said, "but you can count the outstanding track coaches on one hand."

When World War II began, Bill joined the U.S. armed forces and was sent to Europe. Using his athletic talents, he served in the U.S. Tenth Mountain Division, which fought on skis. He also brought along a pair of sneakers. If he had to get somewhere quickly, he reasoned, he would be faster in track shoes than army boots. In Italy, Bill became a war hero, winning a silver star for seizing a Nazi tank.

During World War II, Bill served in the U.S. Tenth Mountain Division, which traveled and fought on skis.

When the war ended, Bill continued coaching track, now at the University of Oregon. After Bill Hayward died—and the University of Oregon track was renamed Hayward Field—Bill stepped into his old coach's shoes and took over the track team.

A Young Coach Builds a Team

Bill did all he could to prepare his runners in advance of a meet. He would film track events, then show the footage to the athletes so they could better understand their strengths and weaknesses. He created a different training routine for each runner, based on individual abilities. When a runner objected to one of the coach's demands, Bill would silence him with one phrase: "You can't win a race with your mouth."

While other coaches nervously stood by the track during a meet, Bill watched from the top of the stands. He was confident that his athletes understood his lessons and could do without him on the field.

Bill always encouraged his runners to work for greatness. When the University of Oregon lost, however, Bill knew how to encourage his runners and keep up the team's spirit.

"Victory is doing the best you can," he often said to his team. "Even if you lose, you will have learned something. Maybe you'll see the need for more physical conditioning, or knowing your competition better, or using different tactics."

Coach Bowerman proudly called his team "the Men of Oregon" and always told them, "You are a cut above average."

Bill liked to experiment, and he was always looking for new ways to help and guide his team. For example, the coach often mixed together a special drink to energize his athletes. He also tried to create a specially designed running shoe that was specifically tailored to Oregon's damp and hard-to-grip tracks.

Making Special Shoes

As a young man, Bill had raced in lightweight metal spikes. But by the 1950s, American companies were no longer making that type of shoe. Bill felt he had no choice but to craft his own special shoes for his top runners. "If you can't find someone to do it for you," he said, "learn to do it yourself."

"Victory is doing the best you can," Bill said. "Even if you lose, you will have learned something."

As the coach at the University of Oregon, Bill designed and created running shoes for his top athletes.

It took Bill about four hours to make each pair. He used old grocery bags to cut out patterns, and kept changing the size and shape until each shoe was suited to each athlete. The finished product was slightly lighter than the racing shoe sold by the German company, Adidas. Although some joked that Bowerman's shoes looked funny, the shoes fit perfectly and helped many runners win races.

The weather in Oregon is not ideal for running. Training in the winter often meant running in the rain. It took an athlete of special dedication to run regularly in these conditions. Although he was far from the best runner on the team, Phil Knight was the type of student who never missed a practice.

Phil's focused attitude impressed Bill Bowerman. Because he liked Phil's spirit, the coach regularly used the runner to try out new hand-made spikes.

Phil marveled at his coach's inventiveness. Years later, he'd remember how a teammate named Otis Davice once put on a pair of Bill's shoes and "beat a runner he had no business beating."

Bill Bowerman and Phil Knight stayed in touch after Phil graduated college in 1959. Phil went to Stanford School of Business, where he was assigned to write a paper on starting a small business. "Write about something you know," instructed his professor, Frank Shallenberger. "And something you like."

Phil Knight wrote about sneakers.

— 3 —

Chasing a Dream

While Phil was working on his paper, Bill Bowerman continued to make his running spikes. Several of his athletes even broke records in the shoes he designed. And, in 1959, he signed a contract with the Spotbilt company to manufacture and sell one of his designs. Unfortunately, when the shoe was finally made, it looked nothing like Bill's design. He felt that the spike they used was no different than any other, and demanded that his name be removed from the shoe.

Meanwhile, Phil was hard at work studying the sneaker industry. Although Adidas made the best sneakers in the world at the time, their price was much higher than American models. Phil decided to investigate the possibility of importing shoes from Japan, where the cost of making the product was lower than in America. Phil believed that, within three years, he could sell more than 20,000 pairs of sneakers annually to high schools and colleges.

Above all, Phil wanted to market a shoe that his fellow runners would truly appreciate. "I had determined...that what I wanted to do with my life was to be the best track-and-field shoe distributor in the United States," he recalls.

Traveling the World

After graduating from Stanford in 1962, Phil took a worldwide tour, making a special stop in Japan. He visited sporting goods stores all over the country and learned that Japan's most popular track shoe was called Tiger. Young Phil met with officials from the company, and claimed to be an established American shoe distributor.

Phil decided he wanted to be "the best track-and-field shoe distributor in the United States."

"What is your company called?" he was asked.

Phil instantly made up a name: "Blue Ribbon Sports." He'd later say the title suggested first place finishes. To further interest the executives, he mentioned that he ran for Bill Bowerman. The Japanese were intrigued: Bill's team had just won the NCAA track-and-field championships.

After returning to Portland, Oregon, Phil found a job working as an accountant. But he continued his relationship with the Japanese manufacturer. In December, 1963, he received five pairs of Tiger sneakers, and immediately sent two samples to Bill Bowerman. He offered to provide the coach with shoes at a discount rate.

But Bill didn't want to simply buy the shoes from Phil. He wanted to get involved in Phil's new business. He arranged to meet his former runner at a Portland track meet, and came up with an idea. Bill proposed to use his athletes to test the Japanese shoes. If he was satisfied with the running spikes, he'd recommend them to other coaches. Plus, he'd furnish Phil with some of his own designs that the Japanese manufacturer could use to develop new, improved styles.

After discussing the proposal some more, the two partners decided that Phil would run the business and Bill would develop ideas. They shook hands, and each agreed to contribute $500 to make Blue Ribbon Sports a reality.

In 1963, Phil and Bill decided to team up as business partners. Their first company was called Blue Ribbon Sports.

Less than a week later, Phil wrote his former coach to say that 300 pairs were already on their way. Customers would be charged $6.95 each—less than Adidas' price. On each pair sold, the partners would make a profit of $2.89.

At the Hayward Relays at the University of Oregon—the country's biggest high school track meet—Phil and Bill began promoting their product. Phil made up fliers that described the special features of a Tiger shoe and Bill made sure that each coach present received the flier.

Phil's parents' house became Blue Ribbon Sports' headquarters. Sneakers were piled high around the furnace in the family laundry room.

Bill had always told his runners, "Nobody ever remembers number two."

Phil's sister Joanne was in charge of sending out orders.

Although the operation was tiny, Phil predicted big things. If the sports shoe business could be compared to a race, Adidas was the front runner. Although Blue Ribbon Sports started out at the rear of the pack, Phil knew that it would one day take the lead. It had to. Bill Bowerman had always told his runners, "Nobody ever remembers number two."

~ 4 ~

Building on an Idea

n 1963, Bill stumbled across an activity that would not only change his life, but the way millions of Americans exercised. His discovery would also be great for his business.

Bill and four of his runners had been invited to New Zealand by Arthur Lydiard, a legendary Olympic track coach. After the athletes competed in races and returned to the United States, Bill stayed behind to exchange training ideas with Lydiard. The New Zealander asked the American if he wished to try a "jog." Bill had never jogged before. But jogging didn't sound as if it would be that hard. He agreed to jog with the coach.

Bill Learns About Jogging

The philosophy of jogging was "train, don't sprain." New Zealanders jogged for conditioning, not competition. They ran at a slow, even pace in order to improve the heart and build lung power.

Bill was surprised to find that he couldn't keep up with Lydiard, who was at least 25 years older. After several days of jogging, Bill had lost ten pounds and four inches around his waist. He decided that this was something Americans needed.

When he returned from New Zealand, Bill began to conduct jogging classes at Hayward Field in Oregon. He emphasized that jogging was particularly good for middle-aged people. As Lydiard had showed, the activity could help people stay young and fit.

Blue Ribbon Grows

In 1965, Blue Ribbon Sports hired its first full-time employee, Jeff Johnson. Johnson and Phil had known each other as competitors. They ran against each other in track-and-field events. And, while Phil was busy selling his imported Tigers, Johnson had been a salesman for Adidas.

As a Blue Ribbon salesman—whenever someone won a race—Johnson gave him a t-shirt with "Tiger" written across it. At the time, no other sneaker company in the United States advertised this way. Now, every time a track meet was held, the top runners would wear their new shirts—alerting the audience to the new brand.

Then, in 1966, Johnson opened up a Tiger store in Santa Monica, California. The store was located between a beauty parlor and an exterminator. The company then got an extra boost when Bill co-authored an extremely popular book on jogging in 1967. The book, *Jogging: A Physical Fitness Program for All Ages,* would eventually sell a million copies.

Despite his publishing success, the coach's thoughts never strayed far from trying to create the ultimate sneaker. When he first sent instructions to the factory in Japan for a marathon shoe composed of leather and other materials, the Japanese had a problem. There was a shortage of leather in the country. As a result, the factory sent back the first nylon running shoe. Phil took a run in the new shoes, and was delighted. His feet felt so

The jogging craze that swept across America helped make Blue Ribbon Sports a success.

light, they practically "swooshed" through the air. Later, the now famous Nike logo—or symbol— would be a swirling emblem known as the "swoosh."

Later, Bill cut up two types of Tigers and pinned the best parts together. He then sent the combination to the factory in Japan. The workers there carefully

Whenever a runner won a race, Blue Ribbon salesman Jeff Johnson would give the winner a t-shirt.

followed Bill's instructions, and a new product was created. Because the 1968 Olympics were about to be held in Mexico City, Bill and Phil wanted to call their new creation The Aztec—after Mexico's ancient Indians.

Unfortunately, Adidas already had a sneaker with a similar name. Bill asked Phil if he remembered

the name of the Spanish explorer who conquered the Aztecs.

"Cortez," Phil said. "Hernando Cortez."

The Cortez running shoe soon became one of Tiger's best-sellers. But Phil still kept a second job, just in case the business failed or the money ran out. While teaching accounting at Portland State University, he fell in love with, and married, one of his students, Penny Parks.

Tigers Take Off

By 1969, high school and college teams all over the country were purchasing Tiger shoes. The company now had 20 employees, warehouses in Boston and Los Angeles, and stores in Oregon, California, Massachusetts, and Florida. The yearly sales were nearly $300,000. In the fall, Phil finally quit his teaching job to work full-time for his company.

By 1969, Bill and Phil decided to do bigger things.

Both Bill and Phil now believed it was time to do bigger things. They decided that they would come up with a new brand of sneakers, their own, original brand—a name no one in sports would ever forget.

~ 5 ~

The Birth of Nike

In 1971, a Portland State University student named Carolyn Davidson was recruited to develop a new sneaker logo. She handed Phil a drawing of a stripe that looked like a rolling check mark. "I don't love it," he smiled and told the young woman. "But I think it'll grow on me."

That is exactly what happened. Over time, Carolyn's logo would remind Phil of the sensational "swoosh" he felt when he tried out the Japanese nylon running shoes for the first time.

Now, it was up to the company's employees to create a name. Many ideas were mentioned, but nothing seemed too exciting. On the night before the shoe boxes were to be printed, Jeff Johnson went to sleep, still unsure. At seven the next morning, he suddenly sat up in bed and began to think about Greek mythology. An idea popped into his head: The winged goddess of victory was named Nike.

Again, Phil wasn't thrilled. But there was no time to waste. "I guess we'll go with the Nike thing for now," he said. "I really don't like any of them, but I guess that's the best of the bunch."

Nike didn't have to look far to locate an expert to endorse its product. In 1972, Bill Bowerman was named coach of the U.S. Olympic track-and-field team. When the country's best runners flocked to the try-outs in Eugene, Oregon,—now known as the "Track-and-Field Capital of the United States"—they heard the Olympic coach speak about the exciting new brand of running shoe.

A Company Searches for an Identity

Phil was certain that promotions were the key to Nike's future. He wanted sports stars to appear in Nike ads. While other companies sought out clean-cut All-American athletes, Nike was looking for a different image. Ilie Nastase from Romania, the first tennis player associated with the company, had the nickname "Nasty" because of his bad temper. But he played with all his heart, and that appealed to Phil. Later on, popular "bad boy" tennis greats John McEnroe and Andre Agassi would also sign contracts with the company.

McEnroe was "the type of player Nike wanted in its shoes—talented, dedicated, and loud," said Ian Hamilton, director of Nike's tennis division. "When I first saw Andre (Agassi), he was a 15-year-old junior tennis star...Even then, image was everything to Andre. He had long hair on one side of his head and no hair on the other. His approach to the game was as it is now—'hit the ball as loud as you can.'"

Naturally, Nike had an easy time attracting many of the world's best-known track stars. Since many of the salesmen were runners themselves, there was an automatic understanding between the professionals and the salesmen. "We...tried to get our shoes on the feet of runners," Phil says. "And we were able to get a lot of great ones under contract—people like Steve Prefontaine and Alberto Salazar—because we spend a lot of time at track events and had relationships with the runners."

Phil wanted to create a different image for Nike early on.

The Waffle Iron Idea

In 1972, Bill made what was probably his greatest contribution to Nike. While sitting at the breakfast table, he began eating waffles and thinking about sneaker soles. Suddenly, he had an inspiration. He

Opposite:
One of Bill's greatest contributions to Nike was his creation of the "waffle sole," which he first made on a waffle iron in his garage.

ran into the garage with the waffle iron and poured rubber on it. With that one idea, Bill created Nike's now famous "waffle sole." Placed on a lightweight shoe, the waffle sole gripped running tracks better than the established ripple sole.

Soon, top athletes began to wear Nikes even when they weren't approached by the company. The world's top-ranked tennis player at the time, Jimmy Connors, wore Nikes. Tennis fans everywhere saw those sneakers on his feet when he won both the U.S. Open and Wimbledon tournaments in 1974.

That same year, the company opened its first American factory in Exeter, New Hampshire. By this time, Nike had grown to 250 employees, and sales had reached $4.8 million a year.

By 1974, Bill was ready to slow down a bit. Now, he wanted to concentrate on raising cattle and spending time at home with his wife. He'd already retired as head track coach at the University of Oregon in 1973. In 1975, he sold most of his holdings in the company, but maintained a ten percent ownership of the business. This way, he could continue to provide recommendations—and inspiration for his old friend and partner, Phil Knight.

~ 6 ~

Ups and Downs

At the beginning of the 1970s, Nike sneakers did not exist. But, by the time the decade ended, Nike was the most popular running shoe in America. In addition to its manufacturing plant in Exeter, New Hampshire, the company had opened factories in Maine, Taiwan, and Korea. Athletes all over the world wore the shoes—Henry Rono of Kenya, for example, set four world track records in Nikes in 1978. Sales for the company in 1979 were at $149 million.

In the 1980s, the progress continued. Alberto Salazar set the world record for the New York Marathon in Nike sneakers in 1981. Twenty-three athletes associated with Nike won medals at the World Track-and-Field Championships in Helsinki, Finland in 1983. At the 1984 Olympics, famous Nike-wearer Carl Lewis captured four gold medals for the United States. Another athlete who was associated with the company, Joan Benoit, won the first women's Olympic marathon. There were now 4,000 Nike employees at various locations around the world to handle the demand for Nike shoes and sports-related clothing.

But all was not as positive as it seemed. Even with all the success, some serious business mistakes were made. "We really hadn't adjusted to being a big company," Phil remembers of those days in the early 1980s.

It took Phil and Nike some time to adjust to being a big company.

One mistake was marketing non-athletic "casual shoes." Phil explains, "We knew a lot of people were buying our shoes and wearing them to the grocery store and for walking to and from work. Since we happened to be good at shoes, we thought we could be successful with casual shoes. But we got our brains beat out." Even Phil looks back now and honestly describes the company's casual shoe as "funny looking."

Hard Times

Between 1983 and 1985, profits fell more than 80 percent. The lowest point came in 1986, when Reebok surpassed Nike as America's number one sneaker company. Nike had to lay off 350 employees. "It was terrible," says Phil. "It's the worst thing that could happen to you in business."

Now, Phil knew he needed to draw on the old lessons Bill Bowerman had taught him back at the University of Oregon. He decided that whatever it took, he was going to find a way to pull back into the lead in this race.

"I began to realize how much it meant to me," he recalls. "If Nike was going to fall, I wanted to be in it up to my eyeballs. I wanted to say I did everything I could to make it work."

The company's rescue can largely be credited to basketball superstar Michael Jordan. In 1985, when he was a rookie with basketball's Chicago Bulls, he signed a deal with Nike.

The Air Jordan sneaker—named after Michael— was designed with a comfortable cushion of air inside it. The shoes were also so colorful that the National Basketball Association (NBA) banned them.

In 1985, the development and promotion of Air Jordans put Nike back on top of the American sneaker business.

Phil remembers that, "Michael Jordan wore the shoes despite being threatened with fines and, of course, he played like no one has ever played before. It was everything you could ask for, and sales just took off."

In fact, Air Jordans brought the company more than $100 million in sales.

A Company Dedicated to Style

Nike quickly became a company dedicated to style. Their sneakers looked different from other brands. And the company's commercials were also a change from what viewers expected. Nike's first television ad was broadcast in 1987. The product it promoted was called Visible Air, a sneaker with a transparent material that exposed the air cushion inside. The music used was a famous Beatles song, "Revolution." Phil said he wanted the commercial to communicate "a revolution in the way Americans felt about fitness, exercise, and wellness."

By 1988, Nike was again America's sneaker leader. Nike's ads encouraged living up to your ambitions with the now famous phrase, "Just Do It." In 1990, the company opened its huge, new head-quarters—called the Nike World Campus—in Beaverton, Oregon. In addition to a basketball gym, tennis court, and jogging track, there were three restaurants, a beauty parlor, a child-care center, and a radio station. The buildings were named after sports heroes, like baseball greats Mike Schmidt and Nolan Ryan, and tennis star John McEnroe. The address of the compound: One Bowerman Drive.

7

Moving Forward

The early 1990s saw athletes associated with Nike enjoy success that few ever imagined. Andre Agassi—a 50-to-1 underdog—shocked the world by winning England's Wimbledon tennis tournament in 1992. At the Olympics that year, every medalist on the U.S. track-and-field team wore Nike clothing. Six members of the "Dream Team"—the U.S. basketball squad consisting of NBA superstars—had contracts with Nike. One of the players was Michael Jordan, who—earlier in the year—led the Chicago Bulls to their second straight NBA championship.

41

Star European athletes also flocked to Nike. Ukrainian pole vaulter Sergei Bubka—a household name throughout the former Soviet Union—also began promoting the company's products.

By the early 1990s, more and more customers around America could go to special Nike stores to buy their favorite sportswear. The first Nike Town— a 60,000-square-foot retail space—opened in Chicago in 1992. A year later, there were similar "super stores" in Portland, Oregon, and Costa Mesa, California. At Nike Towns, visitors can choose from 400 different types of sneakers, and go through what some have described as a "sports museum." There are videos of great games, and large statues of stars like Michael Jordan and Andre Agassi. In the future, Nike plans to build up to 15 Nike Towns in various locations across the United States.

Because of its success, the company is always under pressure to live up to its reputation for entertaining ads. In the commercial that aired during the 1992 Super Bowl, Michael Jordan was seen playing basketball with cartoon character Bugs Bunny. Phil said that it took six months to develop the drawings for the million-dollar advertisement.

Quality Control

Despite all the glitter, most people think of Nike as a sneaker company. And all the fancy ads in the world will not help if Nike starts making inferior shoes. With this in mind, the company employs advanced products engineers, who jokingly refer to themselves by the abbreviation APEs. After the APEs come up with new sneaker ideas, athletes are hired to try out the shoes. In one test, 186 people from Alaska to the Virgin Islands were selected to put some of Nike's products to the test. They were told to walk or run 45 miles a week. Rocks, glass, and other rough surfaces were not to be avoided. The findings were then reported to Nike's main office. The goal was to make sure that all of Nike's shoes would hold up for more than 500 miles.

Today, Phil works hard to make sure Nike products are only of the highest quality.

Today, Nike's original inventor, designer, and tester, Bill Bowerman, continues to keep an eye on the new sneakers that Nike creates, and offer advice. Not surprisingly, he still favors lighter shoes that are ideal for running.

Sadly, Bill's many experiments proved damaging to his health. The toxic (poisonous) fumes from the

Even though Nike is one of the world's most popular and successful companies, Phil and his employees keep a close eye on quality control for all their products.

glue he used while making shoes have blurred his vision and now restrict his walking. Today, he limps and has to use a leg brace.

Despite his health problems, Bill's outlook on life has remained positive. During his retirement, he formed a center for the study of health and fitness at the University of Oregon. He also spent his own money to build an addition to Hayward Field.

The partnership between Bill Bowerman and Phil Knight lasts to this day, even though Bill is not a daily presence in the office. It was Phil's business knowledge that made Nike into the world's biggest sneaker company. But that success would never have been possible if Phil hadn't relied on Bill's important advice and philosophy. Phil will always remember one of Bill's favorite sayings:

"It's not how hard you work," Bill would always say, "it's how intelligently you work."

"It's not how hard you work, it's how intelligently you work." And that's the main idea upon which the Nike empire was built.

Glossary

conditioning Physical improvement; working to get into shape.

exterminator Person who kills insects or pests.

importing Bringing in from another country.

legislature Government body; lawmakers.

logo Visual symbol used to represent a company in the marketplace.

pioneer Person who settles wild or unexplored land.

slogan Catchy phrase, usually used for advertising.

spikes Metal cleats on the soles of running shoes.

Further Reading

Gutman, Bill. *Track & Field.* Bellmore, NY: Marshall Cavendish, 1990.

Menzies, Linda. *Teen's Guide to Business: The Secret to a Successful Enterprise.*New York: Master Media Ltd., 1992.

Merrison, Tim. *Field Athletics.* New York: Macmillan, 1991.

Young, Richard G., ed. *Philip H. Knight: Running with Nike.* Ada, OK: Garret Educational Corp., 1992.

Index

Adidas, 19, 20, 24, 26, 29
Agassi, Andre, 33, 41, 42

Benoit, Joan, 37
Blue Ribbon Sports, 21–24, 26, 27
Bowerman, Barbara (wife), 12
Bowerman, Bill
   childhood, 12, 13
   college, 12, 19
   at Medford High (coach), 14
   in U.S. Tenth Mountain Division,
      14, 15
   at University of Oregon (coach), 6,
      16–17, 18
Bowerman, Lizzie (mother), 12

Chicago Bulls, 38, 41
Conners, Jimmy, 35

Davice, Otis, 19
Davidson, Carolyn, 31

Hamilton, Ian, 33
Hayward, Bill, 13, 14, 16
Hayward Relays, 24

Jogging, 6, 25–27
Johnson, Jeff, 26, 31
Jordan, Michael, 38, 39, 41, 42

Knight, Joanne (sister), 24
Knight, Lota (mother), 10
Knight, Phil
   birth, 10
   childhood, 10
   school, 9, 10, 11, 19, 21

at Portland State University
      (teacher), 30
Knight, William (father), 10

Lewis, Carl, 37
Lydiard, Arthur, 25, 26

McEnroe, John, 33, 40

Nastase, Ilie, 32
Nike
   ads, 5, 32, 40, 42
   annual sales, 7, 35, 36, 38, 39
   founding, 6
   headquarters, 7, 40
   logo, 28, 31
   Nike Town, 42

Olympics, 6, 29, 32, 37, 41

Parks, Penny (wife), 30
Prefontaine, Steve, 33

Reebok, 38
Ryan, Nolan, 40

Salazar, Alberto, 33, 36
Schmidt, Mike, 40
Shallenberger, Frank, 19
Spotbilt, 20

Tiger Shoe Company, 21, 22, 24–30

U.S. Open, 35

Wimbledon tournament, 35, 41